ELEMENTS OF GEOGRAPHY

Weather
David Flint

HEINEMANN

Heinemann Library,
an imprint of Heinemann Publishers (Oxford) Ltd,
Halley Court, Jordan Hill, Oxford, OX2 8EJ

OXFORD LONDON EDINBURGH
MADRID PARIS ATHENS BOLOGNA
MELBOURNE SYDNEY AUCKLAND SINGAPORE
TOKYO IBADAN NAIROBI GABORONE HARARE
PORTSMOUTH NH (USA)

© Heinemann Library 1993

First published 1993
94 95 96 97 10 9 8 7 6 5 4 3 2

British Library Cataloguing in Publication Data is available on request from the British Library.

ISBN 0-431-07230-2 (cased)
ISBN 0-431-07235-3 (paperback)

Designed by Philip Parkhouse
Illustrated by Hardlines: pp.8, 12, 14, 17; Taurus Graphics: pp.22, 23
Printed and bound in China

Acknowledgements
The author and publishers would like to thank the
following for permission to use photographs:
J. Allen Cash Photo Library: p.8; Robert Harding Picture Library: pp.4, 6;
Holt Studios: pp.10, 22, 23; International Weather Productions: pp.16, 26;
Frank Lane Picture Agency: pp.12, 15; Planet Earth Pictures: p.20;
Hans Reinhard/Bruce Coleman Ltd: p.29; Science Photo Library: pp.18, 24;
Frank Spooner Pictures: p.5; David Wodfall/NHPA: p.28; ZEFA: pp.11, 14, 21, 25

Thanks to Lolitta Burton-Hogan for her comments on the original manuscript.

Note to the reader
In this book there are some words in the text which are printed in **bold** type.
This shows that the words are listed in the glossary on pages 30–1.
The glossary gives a brief explanation of words that may be new to you.

Acc 2607   551

This book is to be returned on or before
the last date stamped below.

28 JAN 2000

551
Weather
by

ANDREW MARVELL
SCHOOL LIBRARY
PLEASE RETURN

551

Contents

Why is weather so important?	4
Hot and cold	6
Wind	8
Clouds	10
Rain, snow and hail	12
Fog, dew and frost	14
Highs and lows	16
Thunder and lightning	18
Hurricanes and tornadoes	20
The seasons	22
Forecasting the weather	24
And now the weather . . .	26
What is happening to our weather?	28
Glossary	30
Index	32

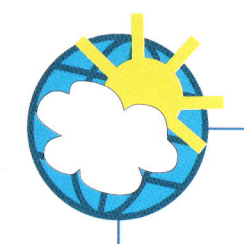

Why is weather so important?

A rainstorm over the hills of the Lake District.

Weather is important to everyone. Every day millions of people check the weather forecast for their area. Knowing about the weather helps us to decide what to wear and what to do. Sometimes changes in the weather can be a matter of life or death.

The weather is often in the news. **Hurricanes** in the West Indies, **drought** in Sudan, floods in the USA and storms in Britain hit the headlines.

Many people need to know what the weather is going to be like. Farmers need to know when to plant and harvest their crops. Airline pilots need to know if they may fly into hurricanes. Sailors need to know if there are dangerous storms at sea. People organizing and taking part in outdoor sports need to know if bad weather is likely to stop the event.

Warnings of bad weather can help people avoid accidents and damage to their property. If heavy frost is forecasted, lorries spread grit on main roads to stop cars skidding. Forecasts of heavy rain mean that people who live near rivers can protect their houses against flooding. If there is a hurricane warning many people leave the danger area.

> **Did you know?**
>
> The sunniest place on earth is the eastern Sahara Desert which has twelve hours of sunshine each day. The least sunny places are the North and South Poles where the sun is not seen for six months of the year.

Scientists have been measuring changes in the earth's weather for over 150 years. They think that the weather is changing – that conditions are getting hotter. People have different ideas about why this is, but most blame **pollution** in the **atmosphere**.

Sports events like tennis at Wimbledon can be affected by bad weather.

Hot and cold

Sun's rays →
Sun's rays →
Sun's rays →

Equator

Some parts of the earth receive more heat from the sun than others.

Temperature is the word we use to describe how cold or hot a place is. We use a **thermometer** to measure temperature in degrees Celsius (°C).

> **Did you know?**
> The highest temperature ever recorded was 58 °C in Libya in 1922.

Some parts of the earth are hot, others are cold. All the earth's heat and light comes from the sun. Some places, however, receive more sunlight than others. This is because the earth is round. The **Equator** receives the sun's direct rays. Places near the Equator are very hot. At the North and South Poles the sun's rays are spread out over a wide area. Places in the far north and south are cold.

Polar areas are very cold even in summer.

○ Build a temperature stand

You can measure air temperature with ordinary household thermometers. This is how to make a temperature stand.

You will need: a wooden stand; four thermometers; four tubes (eg the cardboard tube from inside a kitchen roll); aluminium foil; Blu-Tack.

Cover the tubes with aluminium foil. This reflects sunlight so that it does not heat up the air inside the tubes more than the air outside. Arrange the stand as shown in the diagram and place the thermometers in the tubes. Fix them with Blu-Tack.

1 Does the temperature vary at different heights above the ground? (eg Is the temperature in the top tube higher than that in the bottom one?)

2 What happens if you place the stand on different surfaces (eg tarmac, grass)? Does the temperature vary?

3 What happens if you put the stand in different places? Is the air temperature lower on the shady side of a building?

4 Does air temperature change at different times of day? What is the temperature at 9 am? midday? 2 pm?

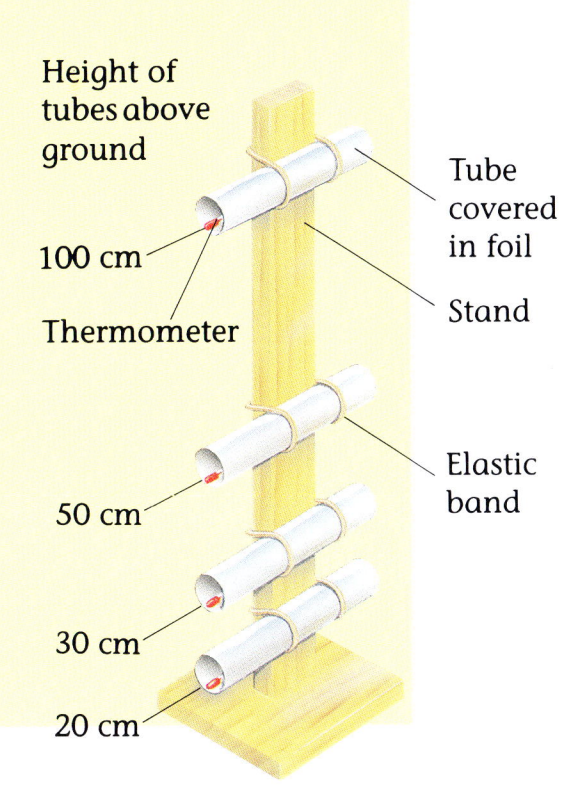

Height of tubes above ground

100 cm
Thermometer
50 cm
30 cm
20 cm

Tube covered in foil
Stand
Elastic band

Wind

Wind is air moving from one place to another. The air around the earth is constantly on the move. It moves across the surface of the earth and up and down in the atmosphere. Sometimes, strong winds from the Sahara Desert pick up dust and blow it thousands of kilometres north to Europe. This red dust settles on cars and can make snow pink!

> **Did you know?**
> The world's windiest place is Antarctica at the South Pole. Wind speeds there often reach over 300 kph.

High winds can bring down trees and cause a lot of damage.

In 1805 Admiral Sir Francis Beaufort worked out a scale for measuring the speed of the wind at sea. He based his scale on miles per hour (mph). He gave each wind speed a number (eg Force 2), a name (eg 'light breeze') and a description of its effects. The **Beaufort Scale** is still used but now it measures wind speed in kilometres per hour (kph).

The Beaufort Scale

Force 1	Light air	(2–5 kph)	Smoke drifts up but **wind vanes** do not move
Force 2	Light breeze	(6–11 kph)	Leaves rustle, wind vane moves
Force 3	Gentle breeze	(12–19 kph)	Leaves and small twigs move
Force 4	Moderate breeze	(20–29 kph)	Dust raised, small branches move
Force 5	Fresh breeze	(30–39 kph)	Small trees sway
Force 6	Strong breeze	(40–50 kph)	Large branches move
Force 7	Near gale	(51–61 kph)	Whole trees sway
Force 8	Gale	(62–74 kph)	Twigs break off trees, walking is difficult
Force 9	Strong gale	(75–87 kph)	Chimney pots blown off
Force 10	Storm	(88–102 kph)	Damage to buildings; trees uprooted
Force 11	Violent storm	(103–120 kph)	Widespread damage
Force 12	Hurricane	(over 120 kph)	Whole area devastated

Clouds

Clouds form when air rises. Air rises for different reasons. Sometimes the air near the ground is heated by the sun. As the warm air rises, the air cools and clouds form. In some places, air is forced to rise over mountains and hills. Again, as the air rises the clouds form.

Air contains moisture called **water vapour**. When air rises it gets colder. The water vapour cools down and **condenses**, that is, it turns into tiny droplets of water. These droplets make the clouds. Clouds are made up of billions of tiny droplets of water or ice. Each droplet is smaller than a grain of flour. They are so small and light that they can float in the air.

These white clouds are called cumulus clouds. They usually bring good weather.

Cirrus clouds.

> **Did you know?**
>
> A bolt of lightning from a rain cloud produces enough energy to run a household light bulb for 10,000 years.

There are three main types of clouds: cirrus (which means 'curl of hair'), stratus (which means 'layer') and cumulus (which means 'heap'). The clouds were given these names in 1804 by a **meteorologist** called Luke Howard. Clouds give us important clues about what the weather will be like. For example, the fine, wispy cirrus clouds tell us that thicker clouds which may bring rain are not far behind. White, fluffy cumulus clouds tend to mean that it will be a fine day.

Rain, snow and hail

Clouds are made up of billions of tiny droplets of water. If the droplets of water in the cloud bump into each other, they join together. So gradually they get bigger. Eventually the droplets become too big and heavy to float in the air and they fall as **rain**. If the temperature of the cloud is below **freezing point** the droplets fall as **snow** instead of rain.

Sometimes rain falls steadily for hours. This happens when the air rises slowly. As the water vapour cools and condenses, clouds are continually made and the rain keeps falling. At other times, rain falls as a short, heavy shower. This happens if the air rushes upwards and cools down very quickly.

Rain is vital to all life on earth. People and animals need water for drinking and washing; plants need water to grow. Droughts occur in places where there is little or no rain. When there is a drought, crops dry up and animals die, so there is no food for people. This is called **famine**.

Snow makes the roads very slippery and dangerous.

○ Make a rain gauge

A **rain gauge** measures rainfall.

You will need: A plastic bottle (eg an empty lemonade bottle), a ruler, sticky tape.

1 Cut the top off the plastic bottle (cut about 10 cm from top).
2 Place the top upside down inside the rest of the bottle. Seal the two parts with sticky tape.
3 Mark a scale showing millimetres on a piece of paper. Use a ruler to do this. Stick this on the side of the bottle.
4 Place your rain gauge outside in an open space. To stop it falling over, place it in the soil. Each morning at the same time, see how much rain has fallen in the last 24 hours. Record your result before emptying the rain gauge.

Hail falls from tall, black clouds. Inside these clouds there are very strong air currents. Raindrops that form inside the cloud are carried up and down by these air currents. At the top of the cloud the air is very cold and the raindrops freeze. Then as they fall more water sticks to them. A drop may travel up and down inside the cloud many times. Eventually the drops fall as lumps of ice made from many layers of frozen water. This is called hail.

Top of plastic bottle
Sticky tape
Scale

➤ Did you know?

The wettest place in the world is Tutunendó in Colombia, South America. Over 11 m of rain fall every year!

Fog, dew and frost

Clouds and rain form when air rises and water vapour cools. Sometimes water vapour cools when it is near cold ground. This is when **fog**, **frost** and **dew** form.

When the ground loses heat, it becomes colder and colder. As the ground cools it also cools the air above it. The water vapour in the air condenses. It forms billions of tiny drops of water. This is fog. Fog builds up in wet, low-lying areas like river valleys.

Fog is dangerous for drivers because it can be difficult for them to see the cars in front. Sometimes they do not slow down in time to avoid a crash.

Mist and fog fill the valley. Higher up the air is clear.

Frost forms during very cold nights. It even builds up on cobwebs.

Dew forms on calm, clear nights. Water vapour in the air condenses onto cold surfaces like roads or the leaves of plants. The droplets of water that form are called dew.

If the temperature of the ground falls below freezing point then frost forms instead of dew. Everything is covered by a thin layer of frost. Frost makes paths and roads slippery, so people walking or driving need to take care.

When the air becomes warmer, the water droplets or ice turn back to water vapour. Fog, dew and frost often disappear once the sun comes out.

> ### Did you know?
>
> Smog is a mixture of fog and smoke particles. Smog used to be a big problem in British cities. Over 20,000 people died in one week during a bad smog in 1952. Now there are laws to control smoke emissions. Smog is no longer a problem in Britain.

Highs and lows

Forecasters point out areas of high and low pressure on their maps.

It may not feel as if air weighs anything at all. But in fact, the air presses down heavily on the earth's surface. This is known as **air pressure**. Air pressure can change. It can be high or low. Changes in air pressure affect the weather.

Areas of high pressure are called **anticyclones**. They usually bring fine weather with some sunshine. In winter anticyclones bring fine, cold weather and there are frosts at night.

Areas of low pressure are called **depressions**. They usually bring cloud and rain. If low clouds form, the rain is usually a heavy **drizzle**. If tall clouds form, there could be a heavy downpour of rain with **thunder** and **lightning**.

The weather maps used by weather forecasters show anticyclones and depressions. By knowing where the areas of high and low pressure are, we have a good idea of what the weather will be like.

Barometers are used to measure air pressure. They show how the air pressure is changing. If the barometer shows that high pressure is coming the weather is likely to be dry. If a depression is on the way it is likely to rain.

> **Did you know?**
> High air pressure can make high tides even higher. This adds to the dangers of flooding at the coast.

A depression brings cloud and rain.

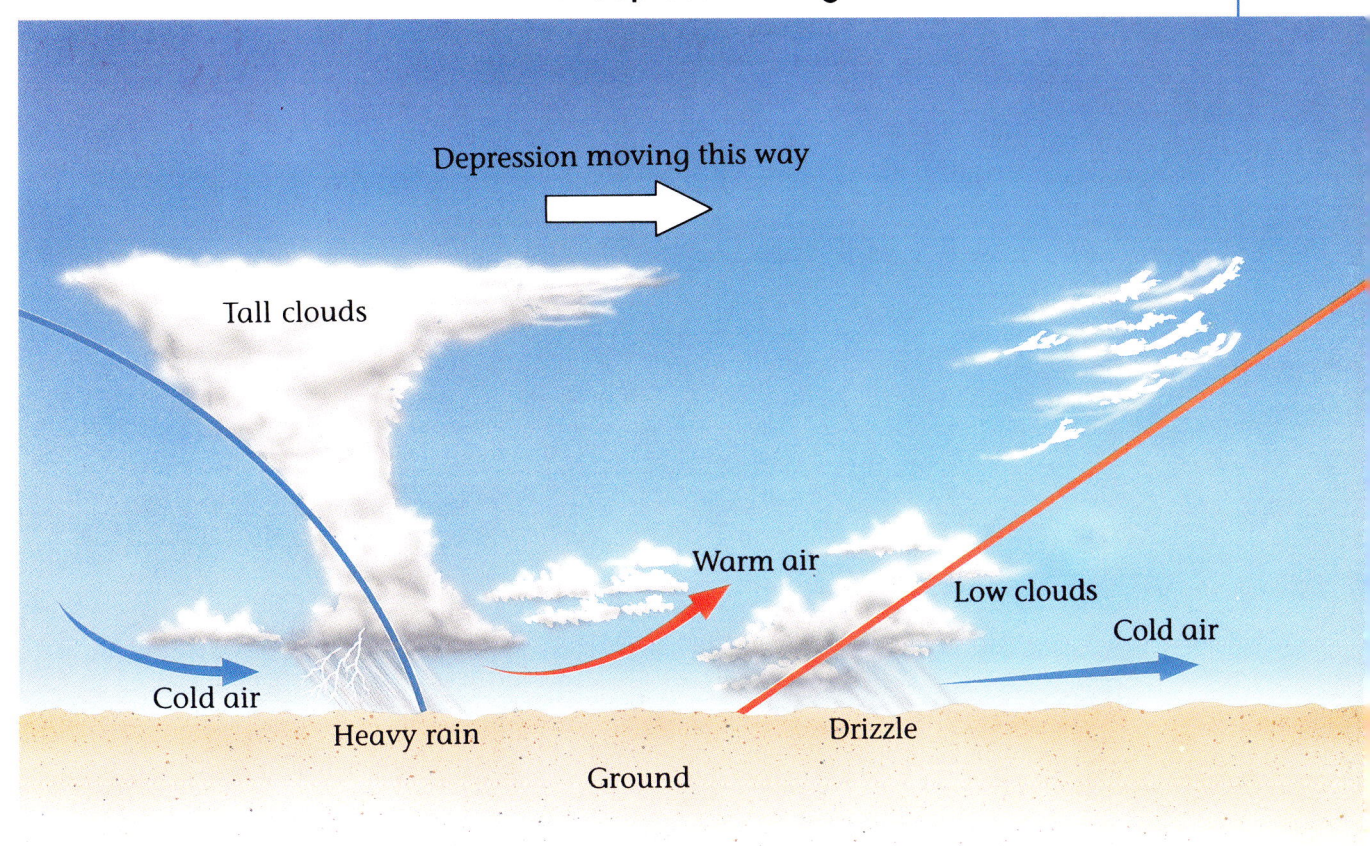

Depression moving this way

Tall clouds

Warm air

Low clouds

Cold air

Cold air

Heavy rain

Drizzle

Ground

Thunder and lightning

Storms with heavy rain, thunder and lightning are called thunderstorms. They happen when warm, moist air rises quickly, for example on a hot summer afternoon. You can tell a thunderstorm is coming when the sky gets darker and tall black clouds appear. Often there is a blast of cool air just before the rain starts.

> **➤ Did you know?**
> You can work out how far away a storm is by timing how long it takes between the lightning flash and the sound of the thunder. A gap of three seconds means the storm is 1 km away.

Thunderstorms often last an hour or more. Sometimes they move away and then come back in a few hours. Close to the Equator, thunderstorms happen almost every day. They usually happen in the afternoon when the heat has built up.

Lightning strikes from the clouds down to earth.

Thunder cloud

Lightning

Church with tower and lightning conductor

Ground

A thunderstorm.

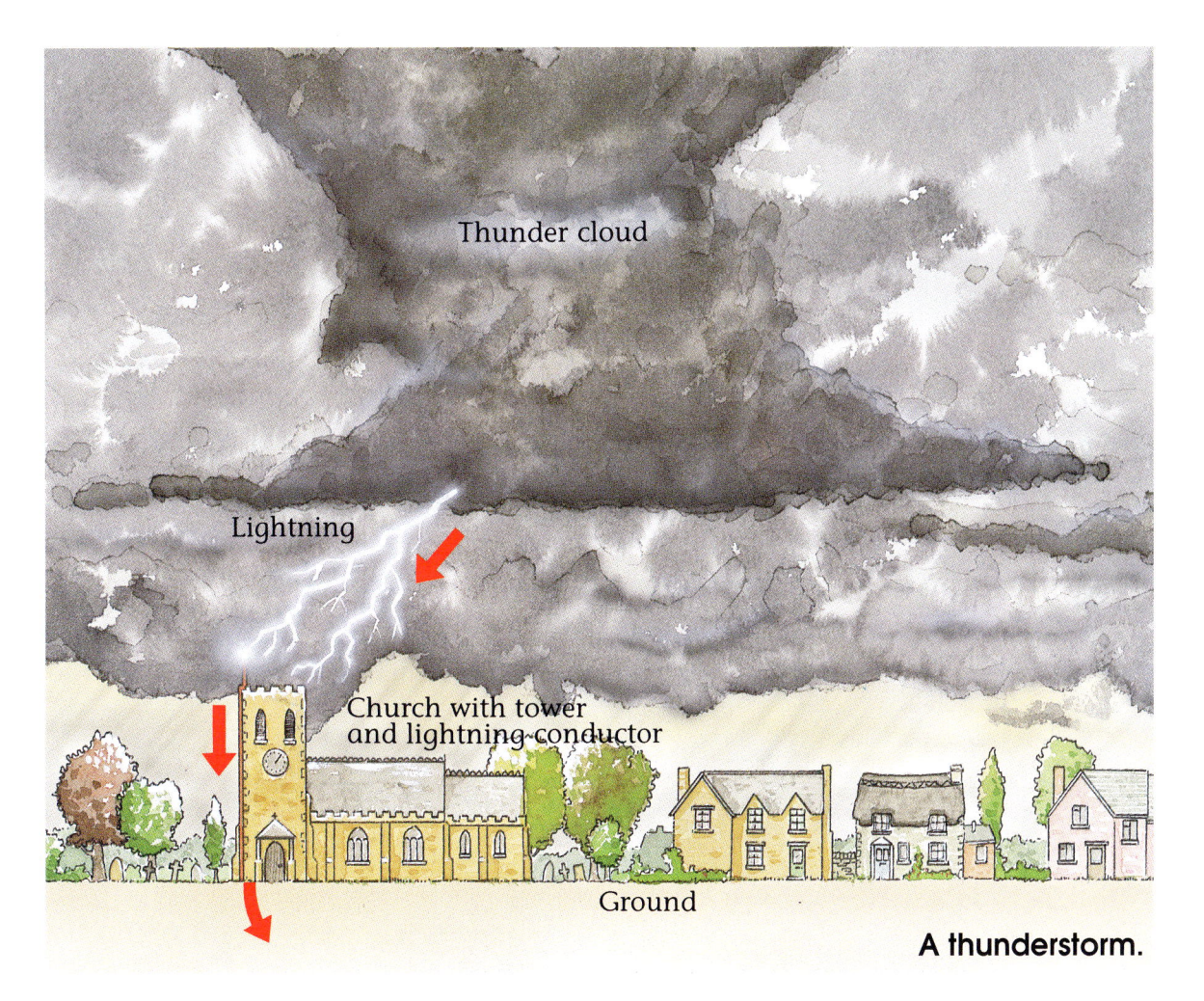

Lightning is caused by electricity in the clouds. This electric charge builds up until lightning sparks across the gap between the clouds and the ground. Sometimes it hits a tall building or a tree and causes a lot of damage. It is dangerous to shelter under a tree in a thunderstorm. Many tall buildings have a strip of copper which runs from roof to ground. This **lightning conductor** carries the electricity into the ground where it will do no harm.

Lightning heats the air it passes through to a temperature of 30,000°C – five times hotter than the sun! The heated air expands quickly. Thunder is the sound of this hot air expanding.

Hurricanes and tornadoes

Hurricanes and **tornadoes** are violent storms. Each year they injure or kill thousands of people around the world. They also cause millions of pounds worth of damage.

> ➤ **Did you know?**
> Wind speeds in tornadoes can be as high as 700 kph. In some tornadoes fish, frogs and other animals have been swept up into the air.

Hurricanes are storms which start over a warm sea, like the Caribbean. Here winds coming from opposite directions meet. Swirls of air form where the winds meet. The air moves faster and faster until it reaches speeds of about 300 kph. This wind is so strong it can demolish houses. It whips up vast waves on the sea which may destroy boats and harbours. A hurricane can generate as much energy in a second as ten atomic bombs! At the centre or 'eye' of the hurricane is a calm area surrounded by strong winds.

Hurricanes last between two and five days. They have different names in different parts of the world. In the Indian Ocean they are known as **cyclones**. In the Pacific Ocean they are known as **typhoons**.

The 'eye' of Hurricane Elena.

The powerful whirling winds of a tornado.

Weather satellites can spot a hurricane building up. Meteorologists give each hurricane a name to help identify it. One year they give the hurricanes male names, the next female, then male again, and so on. The hurricane season starts in September. The first hurricane of the season is given a name beginning with 'A', like Alma or Adam, and so on throughout the alphabet. The world's worst hurricane was in 1970 in Bangladesh. Over a million people died in the storm and the floods that followed it.

Tornadoes or 'twisters' form over land. They last between ten minutes and four hours. They are smaller than hurricanes, but more violent. Usually the centre is about 100 m wide and the whole tornado is about 500 m wide.

The seasons

In most parts of the world the weather changes through the year. Part of the year may be mostly wet and cold with snow and frost. Another part of the year may be mostly hot, dry and sunny. Each period with its own type of weather is called a season. Seasons affect plants, animals and people. In Britain, for example, some crops are planted in the summer and are harvested in autumn. Some animals like hedgehogs hibernate (sleep) in winter when it would be too cold for them to survive.

The North and South Poles have just two seasons. They have six months of winter followed by six months of summer. Other places, like Europe and North America have spring and autumn as well as summer and winter.

The Amazon rainforest lies over the Equator. It has only one season – hot and wet. Sometimes there are drier times, and sometimes there are slightly cooler times. But the weather changes very little over the year.

A country scene in summer.

Most parts of India have three seasons. For part of the year it is very hot and dry. Then in June the monsoon wind starts to blow from the south west. It brings very heavy monsoon rain. This is the monsoon season or the rainy season. After the rain there is a cool, dry season.

We have seasons because the earth tilts. At different times of the year different parts of the earth are close to the sun. In June the North Pole is tilted towards the sun and the South Pole is tilted away from it. This is summer in the northern half of the world and winter in the south. Six months later the South Pole is tilted towards the sun, so it is summer in the south and winter in the north. Places near the Equator receive the same amount of sunlight all year round. This is why they do not have changing seasons.

> **Did you know?**
> Giant hailstones as big as tennis balls fell in Alabama in the USA in April 1988. Some smashed car windscreens.

The same scene in winter.

Forecasting the weather

Weather forecasters are like detectives. They have to put together pieces of information from all over the world. This information tells them what the weather is like now. Then the forecaster has to work out what is likely to happen next.

> ➤ **Did you know?**
> The UK research plane is called 'Snoopy' because it has a long nose that holds measuring instruments.

Forecasters use special equipment to keep an eye on the weather. There are about 10,000 **weather stations** all over the world. These are linked together in a system called 'The World Meteorological Organization'. In Britain there are over 100 weather stations, but another 6000 people (including scientists and amateurs) make weather measurements every day.

This weather satellite picture shows an area of heavy rain over Britain.

A weather balloon being launched up in to the sky.

Every three hours, meteorologists at each weather station record information about the local weather. They record temperature, wind direction, wind strength, clouds, air pressure, **visibility**, **precipitation** (rain or snow), sunshine and **humidity**. This information is sent quickly to regional centres like airports. From here it is sent on to one of the world's main 10,000 stations. Countries are constantly swapping information to try to make sure that their forecast is correct.

Out in space, weather satellites travel round the earth. They send down pictures and information every 30 minutes. They show things which cannot be seen from the ground, for example the air temperature at different heights. Free-flying balloons are sent up to 30 km above the earth. They send back information on air pressure and temperature.

In Britain a network of radar stations tracks the progress of rain across the country. Each radar has a range of 200 km. Weather ships send back reports on conditions at sea. Pilots fly special aircraft, fitted with instruments to measure weather conditions. These planes are flown through all types of weather to gather information.

And now the weather . . .

Symbols show what tomorrow's weather will be like.

Every day all over the world, millions of people tune in to weather forecasts broadcast on TV and radio. Millions more check the forecast in newspapers, or link in to telephone or computer networks. The information for these forecasts comes from meteorological offices. In Britain, information comes from the London Weather Centre and the main Meteorological Office at Bracknell in Berkshire.

> ### ➢ Did you know?
> Supermarkets need accurate weather forecasts to plan the goods they stock. People buy more cold drinks, ice cream and salads in hot weather.

Nowadays it is possible to get up-to-date information about the weather in the local area, the whole country and even other parts of the world. TV, radio and newspapers give this information. People can telephone for a weather report at any time of the day or night. Computer networks like *Ceefax* or *Oracle* give up-to-the-minute national forecasts. Radio 'shipping forecasts' are very important to people like sailors who need to know if a storm is coming.

Most television weather maps are created by special computers. These computers use symbols to show changes in the weather, for example, how rain is expected to spread over the next 24 hours.

The forecast map is based on a special map called a synoptic chart. This chart is drawn by meteorologists using the latest information on wind, air pressure, temperature, rainfall, amounts of cloud and so on. Synoptic charts are mainly used to give short-range forecasts, that is for the 24 hours ahead. Nowadays, accurate long-range forecasts of eight days ahead are possible. Scientists think that by the year 2010 it will be possible to make accurate forecasts for up to two weeks ahead.

Newspaper weather forecasts.

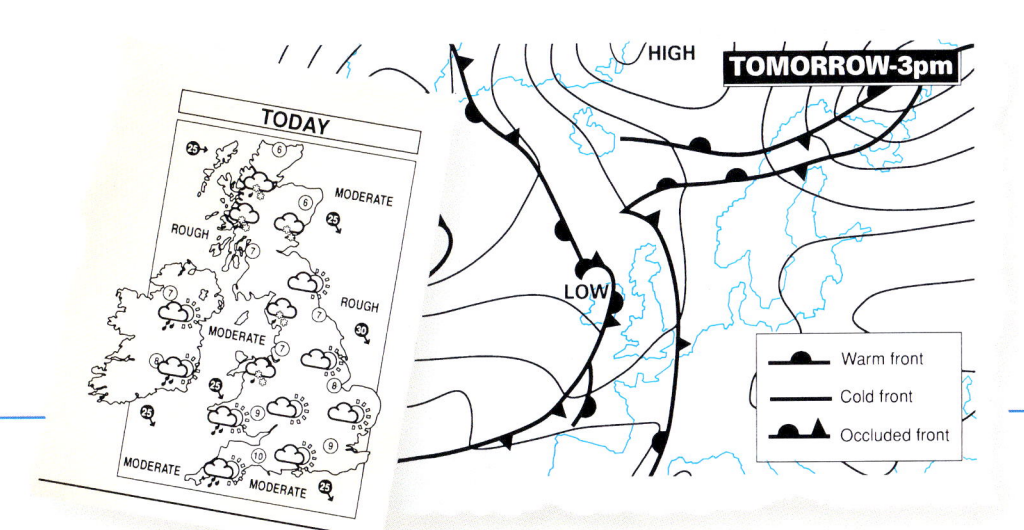

What is happening to our weather?

Accurate records of the world's weather have only been kept for about 150 years. So it is hard to tell if the world's weather is really changing. Most scientists think it is, but they disagree about the causes of the changes and how big the changes will be. Most scientists think that pollution is to blame for changes in the world's weather.

All over the world the temperature seems to be rising. This could be due to the **Greenhouse Effect**. Scientists think it is caused by an increase of gases in the earth's atmosphere. These gases form a layer around the earth. The layer seems to act like a 'greenhouse' by keeping the sun's heat in. Most of these gases come from car and lorry exhausts and power stations. If the temperature goes on rising, the ice at the North and South Poles will start to melt. This will make the sea levels rise. If this happens, many places will be flooded.

Smoke from power stations pollutes the air.

Another effect of pollution is **acid rain**. It was first reported in Scandinavia in the 1970s. Scientists noticed that trees were dying. So were fish in rivers and lakes. Tests showed that the water was acid. This is caused by gases made when coal and oil are burnt. The gases are carried up into the atmosphere and then are spread over a wide area by the wind. The gases dissolve in rainwater and make it acidic. This acid rain damages trees, crops and buildings and pollutes rivers, lakes and streams.

The **ozone layer** is the name given to a blanket of ozone gas about 25 km above the earth. The ozone layer is very important because it keeps out some of the sun's harmful ultraviolet rays. These rays can cause deadly illnesses like skin cancer.

Scientists have discovered holes in the ozone layer. The holes are caused by gases called chlorofluorocarbons (CFCs). The CFCs escape from refrigerators and some aerosol sprays. If the holes continue to grow, more people will develop skin cancer and other diseases.

> ### ➢ Did you know?
> If all the world's ice melted, sea levels would rise by more than 30 m. Vast areas of land, for example parts of the USA and India, would be flooded. Thousands of people could die.

Trees die when acid rain falls.

Glossary

acid rain	Rain that contains dissolved sulphur dioxide and other gases. It causes damage to trees and buildings.
air pressure	The weight of the earth's atmosphere pressing down on the earth's surface.
anticyclone	An area of high pressure in the earth's atmosphere.
atmosphere	The layer of air which surrounds the earth.
barometer	An instrument for measuring air pressure.
Beaufort Scale	A scale of wind speeds.
condensation	The process by which water vapour turns into tiny drops of water as it cools.
cyclone	Another name for a hurricane.
depression	An area of low pressure in the earth's atmosphere.
dew	Droplets of moisture that condense on cold surfaces, often early in the morning.
drizzle	Very fine rain, consisting of drops less than 0.5 mm in diameter.
drought	A serious shortage of water.
Equator	The imaginary circle around the earth, the same distance from both the North and South Poles.
famine	A famine occurs when there is a lack of food for people and animals.
fog	Billions of tiny droplets of water floating in the air near the ground.
freezing point	Temperature at which water turns to ice.
frost	Ice crystals frozen onto a cold surface.
Greenhouse Effect	The warming of the atmosphere due to the sun's heat being trapped by a build-up of gases.
hail	A particle of ice which sometimes forms inside a tall, black cloud.
humidity	The amount of moisture in the air.

hurricane	A very powerful, swirling storm.
lightning	An electrical spark that jumps from cloud to cloud during storms, or from a cloud to the ground.
lightning conductor	Strip of copper that runs from the top of a building to the ground. It stops the lightning from damaging the building.
meteorologist	A scientist who studies the weather.
ozone layer	A screen above the earth that blocks out the harmful rays from the sun.
pollution	Anything that spoils the environment.
precipitation	A general name for any type of water falling from the sky, for example rain, snow, hail, sleet and drizzle.
rain	Liquid drops of water falling from a cloud.
rain gauge	Instrument for measuring how much rain falls.
snow	Ice crystals falling from the sky (called hail if the crystals are joined in a lump).
thermometer	An instrument for measuring temperature.
thunder	The crash of hot air as it speeds through the sky.
tornado	A violent storm which forms a tall funnel of air about 100 m wide.
typhoon	Another name for a hurricane.
visibility	The distance at which people can still see objects.
water vapour	Water in the air in the form of gas.
weather satellites	Satellites in orbit around the earth that monitor weather conditions on earth.
weather station	Place that measures and records weather conditions.
wind vane	An instrument to show the direction of wind.

Index

acid rain 29, 30
air 10, 13, 14
air pressure 16, 17, 25, 30
anticyclones 16, 17, 30
atmosphere 5, 8, 28, 30

barometer 17, 30
Beaufort Scale 8, 30

celsius 6
chlorofluorocarbons (CFCs) 29
clouds 10, 11, 12, 13, 14, 16, 25
condensation 10, 12, 14, 15, 30
cyclones 20, 30

depressions 16, 17, 30
dew 14, 15, 30
drought 4, 12, 30

Equator 6, 18, 30
eye (of a hurricane) 20

flooding 5, 17
fog 14, 30
freezing point 12, 30
frost 5, 14, 15, 16, 22, 30

Greenhouse Effect 28, 30

hail 4, 13, 23, 30
hurricanes 4, 5, 9, 20, 31

meteorologists 25, 31
monsoon 23

ozone layer 29, 31

pollution 5, 28, 31

rain 4, 5, 12, 13, 14, 16, 18, 25, 31
rain gauge 13, 31
rainforest 22

seasons 22, 23
smog 15
snow 4, 12, 22, 23, 25, 31
sun 6, 10, 15

temperature 6, 7, 25
thermometer 6, 7, 31
thunder 16, 18, 19, 31
tides 17
tornadoes 20, 21, 31
typhoons 20, 31

water vapour 10, 12, 14, 15, 31
weather forecasting 4, 21, 24, 25, 26, 27
wind 8, 20, 25
World Meteorological Organization 24